My First Animal Library

Foxes

by Martha E.H. Rustad

Bullfrog Books

Ideas for Parents and Teachers

Bullfrog Books let children practice reading informational texts at the earliest reading levels. Repetition, familiar words, and photo labels support early readers.

Before Reading

- Discuss the cover photo. What does it tell them?

- Look at the picture glossary together. Read and discuss the words.

Read the Book

- "Walk" through the book and look at the photos. Let the child ask questions. Point out the photo labels.

- Read the book to the child, or have him or her read independently.

After Reading

- Prompt the child to think more. Ask: Have you ever seen a fox? What other animals does it look like? How can foxes help people?

Bullfrog Books are published by Jump!
5357 Penn Avenue South
Minneapolis, MN 55419
www.jumplibrary.com

Library of Congress Cataloging-in-Publication Data
Rustad, Martha E. H. (Martha Elizabeth Hillman), 1975-
  Foxes / by Martha E. H. Rustad.
    p. cm. — (Bullfrog books. My first animal library, nocturnal animals)
  Summary: "This easy-to-read nonfiction story tells a "night in the life" of a fox, from waking up, to how they find food and take care of babies, to going back to sleep when the sun comes up"— Provided by publisher.
  Audience: 005.
  Audience: K to grade 3.
  Includes bibliographical references and index.
  ISBN 978-1-62031-069-4 (hardcover) — ISBN 978-1-62496-069-7 (ebook)
  1. Foxes—Juvenile literature. I. Title.
  QL737.C22R869 2014
  599.775—dc23
                                        2013004607

Series Editor: Rebecca Glaser
Series Designer: Ellen Huber
Book Designer: Heather Dreisbach

Photo Credits: All photos by Shutterstock except the following: Alamy 7; Dreamstime 4, 5, 6-7, 8, 14; Getty Images 1; Superstock 9, 10, 13, 21

Printed in the United States at Corporate Graphics in North Mankato, Minnesota.
5-2013 / PO 1003
10 9 8 7 6 5 4 3 2 1

Table of Contents

Foxes at Night

The sun sets. Night begins.

Foxes wake up.

The hungry fox can see in the dark.

His big ears listen.

A mouse
squeaks.

The fox pounces.

8

He brings it to his den.

kit

Mother fox and her kits wait.

The kits play with the mouse.

They learn to hunt.

The foxes eat
the mouse.

They also eat
berries and bugs.

They hunt rabbits
and birds.

The fox buries more food.
A smell marks the hiding places.

His nose finds it later.

A hawk!

The fox barks a warning.

The kits go back to the den.

The fox is tired
after hunting.

He curls up.

His long tail
keeps him warm.

The sun rises.

Day begins.

Foxes go to sleep.

Parts of a Fox

ear
Foxes turn their pointed ears toward sounds.

eye
Sharp fox eyes see in the dark.

snout
A narrow snout reaches food in tight places.

tail
Long tails help foxes balance.

fur
Thick fur keeps foxes warm.

Picture Glossary

den
A home for a fox; foxes often use burrows made by other animals.

kit
A young fox.

hunt
To look for animals for food.

pounce
To jump on something suddenly and grab it.

Index

To Learn More

Learning more is as easy as 1, 2, 3.

1) Go to www.factsurfer.com

2) Enter "fox" into the search box.

3) Click the "Surf" button to see a list of websites.

With factsurfer.com, finding more information is just a click away.